MW00716302

*To*

_____

*From*

_____

Scripture quotations marked NLT are taken from the *Holy Bible,* New Living Translation, copyright 1996. Used by permission of Tyndale House Publishers, Inc., Wheaton, Illinois 60189, USA. All rights reserved.

Scriptures marked NIV are taken from the HOLY BIBLE: New International Version®. NIV®. Copyright © 1973, 1978, 1984 by International Bible Society. Used by permission of Zondervan Publishing House.

Published by Promise Press, an imprint of Barbour Publishing, Inc., P.O. Box 719, Uhrichsville, Ohio 44683  http://www.barbourbooks.com

Member of the
Evangelical Christian
Publishers Association

Printed in China.

# GOD IS IN THE
# SMALL STUFF
## *for* MOMS

# BRUCE & STAN

PROMISE
PRESS
An Imprint of Barbour Publishing

# FAMILY HERITAGE

*The* most personal spiritual celebration you can observe is the spiritual birthday of each family member. What we mean by spiritual birthday is this: On what day did you and others in your family first invite Jesus Christ into your lives? Your spiritual birthday celebrates the number of years you have been a Christ-follower. What better purpose for a celebration can you have? What better reason is there for other people to praise God for your spiritual life? So choose a place and have a party

(presents are certainly optional!).
Invite friends and family, who will
see firsthand the power of God in
the details of your life.

~

*All our life is*
*a celebration for us;*
*we are convinced,*
*in fact, that God is*
*always everywhere.*

CLEMENT OF ALEXANDRIA

~

A family tradition doesn't have to be spectacular or logistically complicated. Sometimes the best traditions are the simplest. A family tradition requires only two components to be successful: It must be celebrated regularly, and everyone in the family must make it a priority.

~

*An* effective tradition in one stage may not work in another. Family traditions can't be forced. They usually happen without fanfare. All of a sudden, you'll find your family repeating a familiar pattern. Find those events and moments. Reinforce them. It will take creativity, energy, and commitment to protect your traditions from the competition of the "outside world," but your family is worth it.

*When* you recall the memories and details and traditions of the house and home you grew up in, think about the memories and traditions you are creating in your own home. That's right. *Creating.* A house is made, not born, and so is a home. What matters about the place where you live is what you put in it every day: the small stuff that will bring your family home long after they've left.

9

# THE
# FAMILY
# HOME

*Happiness* is
to be found only in
the home where God is
loved and honoured,
where each one loves, and helps,
and cares for the others.

THEOPHANES VENARD

~

*The dinner table*
*is the best place*
*for family information,*
*family conversation,*
*and family formation.*

*Lectures* in the living room can be ineffective, but conversations around the dinner table about character, morality, integrity, and behavior are much more palatable between bites of spaghetti. It is around your family's dinner table that each of you will discover a sense of identity—who you are with God, with your family, and with yourself.

*Beauty* is more about style—
your style—than it is about décor.
Collect objects and furnishings
that you and your family can enjoy
because they reflect what your family is all about. Someone should be
able to walk into your home and
connect the small touches with
your family's personality.

*If* God is in your family, then
He should be in your home as well,
through the music that fills your
rooms, the books that line your
shelves, and even the pictures that
hang on your walls. Remember,
it's the small stuff that makes the
difference, whether it's in your life
or in your home.

*Having* guests over for dinner is only part of hospitality—the easy part. The more challenging aspect of hospitality happens the moment the door shuts when the visitors leave. Now the real test of hospitality begins: Can your family treat each other with the same attention and respect that is reserved for special visitors?

~

*With* each kind gesture and display of courtesy, your home will become more like a place you would want to visit and stay for a while. That is what hospitality is all about.

*True* hospitality creates an atmosphere where everyone, family and guests alike, feels special. It make your home a place where visitors want to return and where your family feels comfortable. It makes your house the place where everyone wants to be. They will be at your house because it is a place where they feel appreciated.

~

~

*The world is full
of places to go,
but your home
should be the place
where people
want to stay.*

~

# THE
# SPIRITUAL
# FAMILY

*God* deserves a place in your family, and it is first place. And your family deserves to know God is real and personal. They need to know that He is vitally interested in the events of their lives. . .from the major events to the minor circumstances.

~

*If you keep
God outside
of your family,
there will be
problems inside
your family.*

*Don't* let a day go by without reading the personal and intimate message that God has written for you. As you look at your Bible on the shelf, hear the voice of God whisper, "You've got mail."

~

*God can speak
to you
through the Bible,
but you can't
hear Him
if you keep
the cover closed.*

*Your* personal family is not perfect, and your church family won't be either. But all the good aspects God intended for a family can be found in a church. That family is not complete without you, and you aren't complete without them. That's the way God designed it.

*He cannot have God for his father who refuses to have the church for his mother.*

ST. AUGUSTINE

*Remember* that if the church only admitted people who didn't need it, you couldn't attend either. If a few people irritate you, view them as opportunities to practice the godly virtues of patience and forgiveness and love.

~

# FAMILY
# FUN

*A* sense of humor can be a secret formula for success in your family. Laughter softens the rough edges in the relationships between family members. When your family is laughing together, all of the barriers that might separate them seem to disappear.

*There is no loneliness*
*in a home*
*filled with laughter.*

*Laughter* and weeping
are the two intensest forms
of human emotion,
and these profound wells of
human emotion are to be
consecrated to God.

OSWALD CHAMBERS

~

*Right* living starts with right thinking, which is another way to look at wisdom. That's why the Bible says:

*Fix your thoughts on what is true*
*and honorable and right.*
*Think about things that are*
*pure and lovely and admirable.*
*Think about things that are*
*excellent and worthy of praise.*

PHILIPPIANS 4:8 NLT

~

*Above all else,*
*guard your heart,*
*for it affects*
*everything you do.*

PROVERBS 4:23 NLT

~

# FAMILY
# RELATIONSHIPS

Think about the transformation that can occur in your marriage if you both attempt to be God's servant to each other. No longer will your marriage be characterized by vicious sarcasm or ridicule. Instead, each of you will be looking for opportunities to help the other.

*Try to see yourself
and your spouse from
God's perspective.
It will change the way
that you live.
It will change the way
you love.*

*Babies* don't become physically healthy, emotionally balanced, spiritually sensitive, and personally enjoyable little people on their own. It takes a family to attend to the small stuff in a baby's life. It takes a family to introduce that little person to God and His goodness. And it takes a family to teach that little one that God not only cares, but also wants to get involved in the details of his or her life.

*Expectations* for teenagers:

- Expect your teenagers to make mistakes.
- Expect your teenagers to learn from their mistakes.
- Expect that your teenagers won't tell you everything.
- Expect that you will be informed about the "who, what, where, and when" away from home.
- Expect that you won't be your teenager's best friend.
- Expect to be treated with respect.

*Families* need a third generation. There needs to be a relationship between grandparents and grandchildren. That third generation brings stability, balance, and strength to the family.

*Don't* despair if death or distance has robbed your family of that "third generation." There are many "grandparents" who are waiting to be adopted. You can find them in your neighborhood or in your church. The adoption process is easy. It can get started at the dinner table or with a trip to the zoo.

⁓

*Before* He formed the universe, God knew the day when your child would be leaving home. He has great plans to work in the life of your child—plans that require you to "let go." You need to do your part, so God can finish His part.

~

*"Letting go" means
shifting from
instruction
to influence.*

*You* can pray about your child's future. Pray that God will guide both of you in learning, understanding, and enjoying the evolution of your relationship. Pray that you can move gracefully from rule maker/enforcer to advice-giver. Pray that your mouth will move only after your ear has listened. Pray that God will change your language from *instructions* to *advice*.

# FAMILY
# CHALLENGES

*Conflict is
never easy to deal with,
but when it's resolved,
the bond between
family members is
stronger than ever.*

*The* primary source of conflict, according to God's Word, comes from within us. That's where the envy and selfishness originate. If we realize that, we can better deal with our own "evil desires"—even the small ones—by asking God to forgive us and help us truly love those who are closest to us.

~

*The* tough times you endure can also be a way to prepare and equip your children to handle difficulties in their future. You wouldn't want your children to succumb to their problems with whining and self-pity, so don't let them catch you responding to your troubles that way. Your perseverance in the face of adversity is a lesson your children need to learn, and you can be the best teacher.

*We* have a God Who is in the business of restoring relationships. The most important relationship is ours with Him. While we can reject Him quickly and frequently, He is always ready to forgive and receive us back into fellowship with Him. He never abandons us. He never quits on us. He never gives up on us.

God's unconditional love is
the model He
wants us to use
for marriage.
So, in our age
of disposability,
let's not look at
marriage as some-
thing that can be
discarded or recycled.

# FAMILY
# RESPONSIBILITY

*Responsibility* is a character trait that will produce strong families (and a strong society). But responsibility doesn't happen by accident. It isn't acquired from a parent's wishful thinking or good intentions. Responsibility comes as the result of years of character training. It is developed gradually. If it is not nurtured in your home, you will be stunting your child's growth.

*Honesty* in a family is an amazing thing. When family members are truthful with each other in love, special bonds develop that can never be broken. Honesty is like some kind of superglue that keeps a husband and wife, parents and children, and brothers and sisters closely knit and very much in love.

~

*An honest answer
is like a kiss
on the lips.*

PROVERBS 24:26 NIV

$\mathscr{A}$ loving home fosters encouragement. In that type of environment, your family will feel secure and appreciated. When a loving attitude pervades the home, each family member is encouraged without words even being spoken because they have a sense of self-worth. They know they are loved by their family and by God because of who they are and not because of what they have accomplished.

*As* you think about encouraging your family, don't rely just on words. Look for other ways to communicate what you want to say. Remember, sometimes your heart needs to speak louder than your mouth.

~

*Take* heart!
Your consistent,
loving discipline will
ultimately teach your children
to discipline themselves.
Then your job
will be easier.

~

*Early discipline*
*averts future*
*disaster.*

*Freedom is
the ability to
make decisions.
Wisdom is
the ability to make
the right decisions.*

*Living* a life of good spiritual choices isn't easy, but God has given us the two most important tools we need: His Word and prayer. When you read the Bible, you will discover how to make good spiritual choices, and you'll reap the benefits of good spiritual consequences. When you pray, you will discover that nothing is too small for God to care about.

*Beauty* is all about us,
but how many people
are blind to it!
People take little pleasure
in the natural and quiet
and simple things of life.

PABLO CASALS

~

*Spectacular* things don't happen very often, but the small stuff happens all the time. And when you begin to see God in the small stuff of your family life, then they will become spectacular.

~

## About the Authors

**Bruce Bickel** is a lawyer and **Stan Jantz** is a marketing consultant. But don't let those mundane occupations fool you. Bruce and Stan have collaborated on fifteen books, with combined sales of more than a million copies. Their passion is to present biblical truth in a clear, correct, and casual manner that encourages people to connect in a meaningful way with the living God.

Bruce and his wife, Cheryl, live in Fresno, California; they are active at Westmont College where Bruce is on the Board of Trustees and their two children attend. Stan and his wife, Karin, also live in Fresno; they are involved at Biola University where Stan is on the Board of Trustees and their two children attend.

Contact Bruce & Stan at:
www.bruceandstan.com

# AVAILABLE
# WHEREVER BOOKS
# ARE SOLD

256 pages each; $12.99